*Harmonize Your Purpose!*

# Power to Push You

Parice C. Parker

## *Harmonize Your Purpose!*

Power to Push You
Copyright © 2016 by Paice C. Parker. All rights reserved.

No part of this publication may be reproduced, stored in a retrieval system or transmitted in any way by any means, electronic, mechanical, photocopy, recording or otherwise without the prior permission of the author except as provided by USA copyright law.

Scripture quotations, unless otherwise indicated, are taken from the *Holy Bible, King James Version*, Cambridge, 1769. Used by permission. All rights reserved.

The opinions expressed by the author are not necessarily those of Fountain of Life Publisher's House.

Published by Fountain of Life Publisher's House

P. O. Box 922612 Norcross, GA 30010
Phone: 404-936-3989
Please Email Manuscripts to: publish@pariceparker.biz
For all book orders including wholesale email:
sales@pariceparker.biz
To request author email: author@pariceparker.biz
www.pariceparker.biz

Fountain of Life Publishing House is committed to excellence in the publishing industry. The Company reflects the philosophy established by the founder, based on Psalm 68:11, *"The Lord gave the word and great was the company of those who published it."*

*Book design copyright © 2016 by Parice C Parker. All rights reserved.*
*Cover Design by Parice C. Parker*
*Interior design by Parice C. Parker*
*Editor: FOLPH Editor's Team*

Published in the United States of America
ISBN: 978-0692667439
03.11.2016

# Power to Push You

*Harmonize Your Purpose!*

# Power to Push You

## Table of Contents

Introduction ................................................... 6

Impetuous Zeal …............................................ 7

Follow Your Heart …...................................... 20

Chasing After What Matter's ….................... 27

Let Your Heart Beat At Work …................... 34

Your Destiny Is In Your Purpose ................ 66

If I Can You Can Relocate …....................... 88

Be Persistent …............................................. 93

Run Conqueror Run ….................................118

### Parice C. Parker

*Harmonize Your Purpose!*

# Power to Push You

### *Introduction*

So many people don't know how to flow in their heart desires. It causes a rhythm that will make your heart beat and won't stop until it pumps production out of you. You must know how to flow in life with prosperity, happiness, and goodness.

It's much easier to handle one thing at a time because too much can cause your life to sound like clicking brass, offbeat, and terrible noise. Where there is harmony you will find peace, relaxation, happiness and a prosperous life will begin to flow. It's time to harmonize your purpose.

**Parice C. Parker**

*Harmonize Your Purpose!*

# Chapter One
*Impetuous Zeal*

*S*top *trusting your inner spirit to be fed junk, and sugary knowledge that decapitates your destiny. When you receive the wrong information, you will prolong living life in a messed up situation and have an inverse transformation. Remember, as your soul is prosperous then you will prosper too. If your soul is down, oppressed or stressed then you cannot accomplish your goals. Life is so worth living when you experience the goodness of life. So many have lived in dangerous conditions for so long, they don't know how to live a healthy and*

### *Harmonize Your Purpose!*

*productive life. If your mind is not in a healthy state, then your life will remain chaotic. You can only get out of life what you are willing to invest: including your surroundings, people, things and places. Yes, your environment matters, and it's time you put a fence in your mind that states, "NO TRESPASS!" You cannot allow everything and everyone around you when you are climaxing to an IMPETUOUS ZEAL! It's your push to excel!*

*A very touchy subject that most people don't admit, but people cheat themselves out of having a prosperous life, due to them cheating themselves of keeping their words. Just imagine all the times, for example, you said, "you were going to exercise." What if, you would have kept your word, and how would your body look by*

## Harmonize Your Purpose!

now? Perhaps, the times you said, "you was going to save some money?" If you would have kept your word? How much would you have saved by now, including the interest? Um, I bet a nice lump some of the cash probably enough to invest in your dreams or your children hopes by now. It is so important to begin keeping your word because you hurt more than you. It's your children, family, and friends you become a stumbling block. If you lie to yourself, you only lie to your destiny. Also, it destroys your increase, lowers your self-esteem and assassinates dreams. It's vital to hear what I am saying. My eldest son woke up for years each morning, say, "Mamma are we rich yet?" I often wondered boy what are you seeing? As years passed, I begin to work on more vision, and I was for sure I would soon be

### *Harmonize Your Purpose!*

*rich. Nevertheless, more years of suffering, trying times and fading dreams passed but I still would not quick trying.*

*I have noticed, we hold so many people back in life by being their stumbling block, and causing others not to move forward. Our slothfulness, fear and not moving forward at a firm paste causes others to get distracted and redirected. I could not imagine my life if I would have been the same person I was in 2006. At that time, I was in the beauty industry. I told one if I would have stayed there I would have missed out on my destiny. An absolute, new life was waiting for me and years; I held on to the old and prolonged years of agonizing pains. So many don't realize they could have achieved. Sometimes you feel like you have outgrown your life, and you are not happy. I know*

## *Harmonize Your Purpose!*

*that feeling because I have been there. I just can't take this life anymore and sooner than later misery becomes your everyday mood. So many think that things and stuff will make them happy, but it's your passion for a fulfilled desire that does. It means the world to you. As I was in conversation with her, she was being inspired.*

*When you fix your mind on the power to excel and purpose to hit the target, then it is a done deal. Your goal is now to achieve. No one, nothing or tiredness could stop you now. Power to Push You is missioned to cause you to be an eye specialist. Your eyes will begin to see the benefits of vision; the aspirations once accomplished, and you will have an IMPETUOUS ZEAL. No one can dream for this vision as you or push it in the manner you can and stay focused as you. Vision is*

### Harmonize Your Purpose!

the power to drive people but first one must see the fullness, must feel the passion for it to live and have an IMPEMTEUOS ZEAL to birth it.

Vision is a life modifier and life decorator. It can give you a complete makeover from inside out. Also, when others see it, they will want to be a part or some of what you have. Your success will cause others to desire a much better life and give others a fresh hope to accomplish.

At times, an IMPETUOUS Zeal will cause you to make impulsive decisions, and there is no time to think. I formerly owned Reesie's Hair Palace & Barbershop and Simply the Best Hair Gallery. I couldn't imagine life without Fountain of Life Publisher's House because this vision is why I have a purpose to live. However my I was faced with an impulsiveness one day and my

## *Harmonize Your Purpose!*

*response to many seemed careless when I made my decision move and leave it all behind. Many didn't understand me and at times, I didn't either, but I was driving passionately to see, no longer visualizing my vision as a mere dream, but I had to proceed. And, currently, where I lived wasn't the place to birth my fullness. We all have a call upon of a creative assignment that will define our existence. It's a commission to help better people, places, things, all due towards economic growth and without it, their would be no prosperity or innovation. Our purpose is to cause success. We are to multiply.*

*Awe ... following my heart is the best move I ever made in my life. It takes self-discipline, determination and courage you never had. You must operate in an IMPETUOUS ZEAL. I remember when I lived an unhappy life. I was just*

## *Harmonize Your Purpose!*

*miserable. I would inspire my clients when I had my salons. I told them to follow their heart, and many did. I begin to notice their life was moving forward; happiness was springing up, and purpose was taking place. Wow, I gave advice for others to follow, but I didn't take heed until later. So, one day I realized no more being unhappy or miserable. It was time to relocate my geographical location, change my career and start a fresh beginning. I finally listened to my heart, and all I could see was books, writing, songs and the gift of writing drew my into my Divine Purpose, but I had to push with an IMPETUOUS ZEAL.*

*My new direction was in my heart, and all I had to do was follow it. As I moved forward in life, I came across some difficult times, went through terrible storms and made uncompromising decisions. All I knew was to follow my heart because I could not allow what*

## _Harmonize Your Purpose!_

my eyes was seeing to misdirect my path, hinder my progressive move or change my focus.

Power to Push You is a collaboration of Parice C Parker Phonemically inspiring books. It's like a Divine sampler of vigorous Power to Push You. I want you to move directly into position once you this powerful book. It has the potential to enthuse powerfully you to gain, triumph, tread down, build up and with an IMPETUOUS ZEAL. Power to Push You holds the key cut to unlock all your inheritance because as you read this book procrastination will no longer exist in you. Discover what is in your heart and once you recognize your heart desire, you will start to flow. I am an inspirational author; that's what flows out of me. It's a strength I have, and I was born with it. You have to know your flow and

### *Harmonize Your Purpose!*

*what moves you because that is what will cause harmony in life.*

*No longer shall you deprive you, your family and your friends of being prosperous." 3 John 1:2 Beloved, I wish above all things that thou mayest prosper and be in health, even as thy soul prospereth." I will never forget this conversation I had with someone and I were telling them, "we derive our happiness," and I have the power to let people in my life that are prosperous. The choice is yours whom you allow in your life because they will bring good or cause bad things to happen. Take a good look at them a picture their life as yours. Now, do you still want to be around them? Answer this question because it's deeply imperative. The key to prosperity. Now are you*

## _Harmonize Your Purpose!_

_ready to upgrade your life because as it improves your associations does too. It is something how people scandalize you then wonder why you won't answer their calls. I trust some people in my life and they turned out to be snakes, Jezebels, and so many other things. In my past, I have been too nice to some, smile and keep on going knowing you have bewronged me. Now, I will not tolerate anyone that degrades my character, spread rumors and try to tear up what God would have me to vision. There are times and a season for everything but THIS SEASON IS A NO TOLERANCE TIME that I have adopted forever. I know when God sends it's for the benefit, and that is the life I chose to live... The Good. I don't have time to waste because my GOD ALMIGHTY has been too good to me and there_

### Harmonize Your Purpose!

are so many that want to experience THE GOOD LIFE TOO. GET SERIOUS ABOUT, WHO YOU LET IN, ... everybody is NOT WELCOME HERE.

Some bridges are meant to be torn down to keep people from trespassing. I once heard Will Smith in this television interview, saying, "People burn their bridges too soon." I will never forget it because it entered my spirit immediately though it took years of resignation. By me being in ministry I allowed many to take my kindness for granted but one day I arose and began to allow the bridge to burn because they set they fire. So, why put it out trying to rekindle something meant to die? For years, I would let people in and out my life as if it was a revolving door with no limitation. And, when those people were in my life it was always a

## *Harmonize Your Purpose!*

*disturbance, theft of some sort even if it was my peace and wrongful intentions. Put up your sign and don't take it down, NO TRESPASS! IMPETUOUS ZEAL is gearing up in you; I can feel it. This is the purpose of Power to Push You.*

*Harmonize Your Purpose!*

# Chapter Two
*Follow Your Heart*

When *your days turn into night and your nights turn into nightmares, "What do you do?" So many feel they deserve a much better life and are no longer satisfied with life as it is. Now it is time to put forth that same effort to increase your capabilities. It is time to take a deep look at you. I ask you this question. "What's in your heart?" Getting to know yourself is one of the most difficult things you will have ever to face. The one person you can never run from is you. One person, you see every day is you. So it is required that you change because you cannot run away from yourself. Transformation is expressed through many different things in life. Life transformation is more during critical times or*

## *Harmonize Your Purpose!*

*when a person zeal is cranked up to overdrive; forcing the old you to be more powerful, and then you will begin to operate in a new strength. You are the only one that could love you so much until a change takes place.*

*I have counseled people in my lifetime to become greater. I was a cosmetologist for years and reach so many hearts. A lot of individuals listened to me and took the advice I gave them. For years I counseled them privately as I serviced their beauty needs, not realizing the impact I had in their lives. Some furthered their education, started new businesses to become more successful, but most of all transformed their wealth. Furthermore, all followed their heart. You must look into your heart and find out what can keep your heart in a healthy position. What causes it to beat? Notice, as heart beats there is life. So figure*

## *Harmonize Your Purpose!*

*what is in your heart and give life. Life changes things. Are you a life changer or do you need a change in your life? Transformation is never easy because the change must come from within. Now, the time has come for you to follow what's in your heart. By any and all possible means persevere, until you make that change happen.*

*During transformation the old, you will be exchanged for the new, and it is a process. I know every day you look in the mirror and see a very familiar person looking back at you. Who are you? You saw things in you that no one else sees. You have noticed things about you that no one else is able. Who is that stranger looking back at me? You just cannot figure yourself out, even though you thought you knew. The transformation begins when you start noticing yourself change. You are no longer willing to be that person you used to be*

## *Harmonize Your Purpose!*

*because you desire a change and deserve a better life. You know your past, and it is nothing to relive again. Now, you are ready to know your tomorrow because you realize there is more hope ahead. Is God identifying you to be greater? Your life has scrutinized; your heart played with, and your essence has gone astray. Simply ask yourself the question. Who am I?*

*You have allowed the perception of so many people to make you appear less than what you are purposed to be. You have heard your cries, felt your tears and been victimized many times in your life. You have wrestled with yourself to be more. You have shared your deepest and darkest secrets with you. You also have trusted you with your entire life and have ridden every thriller life roller coaster ride with you. You cannot even get rid of you because for the life you are stuck with*

### *Harmonize Your Purpose!*

*every part of yourself. You have tried to push you away, but you would not budge. Nevertheless, you have tried motivating yourself to do better, but you were discouraged. You know that person in the mirror deserves a far better life, and your dreams are worth living. You have seen how others have abused and used you. Too many have taken you for granted. You have done all you can to satisfy everyone else, and now it is simply time you appreciate you. One day I was sitting in church and as Bishop L D Parker preached about the 30, 60 and 100 fold; immediately, I heard the voice of the Most High and the question was "What fold are you?" I know many people have heard the message about the seed sowing, but that day reality clicked on. Thought in my mind clicked, and reality forced my heart to motivate I am to exist. That day I begin to prepare as never before to raise the value of my life, so I can add*

## *Harmonize Your Purpose!*

more value to others. What fold are you? The fold represents your worth. Is your life value appreciating or depreciating, because one or the other is happening? Do something amazingly good to cause you to become a better you.

Your former life is now history and tells the old you goodbye. Get a new identification (I. D.). Your past has caused a new formula in your life, and it is better than you ever had. The life you desire is breathtaking, and your life will have a whole new definition. Life is a terrible thing to waste, and a lot of people do it every day. I have been one in that number wasting valuable time, days and opportunity to increase my life. We all are found guilty of wasting time, but it does not have to continue. A deficit occurs when value begins to depreciate, or nothing is happening. Therefore, when a loss takes place in life, it is

## *Harmonize Your Purpose!*

*because the value has lost somewhere. Value is priceless when one appreciates the interest of growing. Through the years, many forget to be grateful for the opportunity, and that is why the loss is so devastating. You must take the time to appreciate the opportunity to become all you can. Do not waste another opportunity of reaping the benefit of a 100 fold cultivator. Simply ask yourself the question again, "Who am I?*

*"This chapter "Follow Your Heart," is from my book, "From Eating Crumbs to Transforming Wealth." It is inevitable! This book takes you on a profound journey for revealing change, making you more aware and causing a dynamic effect to inspire a right now transformation. Order your copy today "From Eating Crumbs to Transforming Wealth." at www.pariceparker.biz*

*Harmonize Your Purpose!*

# Chapter Three
*Chase After What Matters*

The best advice that I have given returned more favorably was to follow your heart. So many people miss a life changing opportunity because they burned out in life stopped dreaming and gave up. If you do not keep your desire in front of you, then your dreams will never come true. Also, if you do not continue the upkeep of feeding your hope, then your dreams will die. A man without vision shall perish. Keep chasing after what matters to you regardless of how fooled you look to others. Keep hunting, after all, your dreams and soon they will be in your review mirror.

## *Harmonize Your Purpose!*

*Listening with your heart to hear what motivates you to run. Every runner needs a race and a purpose to run, but one must prepare for the journey. Life has a strange way of equipping us for our life journey, but we must pay attention to what life is speaking to us. Through the years, I heard the voice of much speaking greatness about what they see in me and others inspiring me to go further. God places people in your life for a good reason and sometimes even if the intentions seems to be wrong. There's still a message for you. Listen, because life is speaking your next direction. I know God placed many people in my life, and some caused me to be more sharpened. To chase after what matters you need to know your direction and be prepared not to miss an opportunity when it knocks.*

## _Harmonize Your Purpose!_

*The power of the author in you deserves to exist, but only you have the authority to push that author out! What if Facebook did not exist many relationships would have never formed or businesses took off in the manner they have. What if Alex Haley would not have written Roots we would not have the opportunity of seeing such significant history? And, what if our LORD would have never said: "Let There Be Light"... there is a power that grants opportunity through you! But, the question is whose Opportunity Are You Causing a delay because you have not completed your creative work assignment? The Birth of An Author Shall Be Born – is it you?*

*I heard Bruce Lee say in an interview, "You better train every part of your body." Note, building something bigger than you has never*

## *Harmonize Your Purpose!*

been accomplished. You must tone your entire being to be confident in the completion of your work. Imagine if you were a coffee cup. You can hold all sorts of drink - just an enjoyable part of serving a purpose. A plastic cup will melt if the drink is too hot but a coffee cup can serve more purpose. Nevertheless, if a cup is cracked, it will leak out. So, therefore, you must build yourself an area to tone your weak area in writing, marketing and gaining recognition. Your work is only as valuable as you make it. The percentage you put in is the investment you will receive. There is a compelling author in you. Yes, chase what matters and apprehend your dreams. Go bigger, think bigger and be bigger. No one can make it happen as you can. When You Are Running, Don't Stop! I traded my TV shows and swapped

## Harmonize Your Purpose!

them for a purpose. Every time I wanted to look at TV I wrote in a book, then I completed it. When my BUSINESS ENDED, I was able to MAKE MONEY from book sales. Imagine what you can accomplish when you FIND THE TIME TO WRITE!

- Write 30 Minutes A Day

- Discipline Yourself To Finish One Chapter A Week

- Take Your Book On TOUR

- Increase Your Wealth & Get In Control Of Your Life.

The BEST Life EXPERIENCE is when you can live a meaningful PRODUCTIVE and healthy life. Time and chance happen to all but the key are

### *Harmonize Your Purpose!*

*to be ready for your opportunity. You better be available for your opportunity.*

*The greatest failures are the greatest successors. After putting your heart in your new book the real life begins. Surround yourself with people who believes in you. Be creative in marketing you because without passion pushing your drive you will not make it. Passion is something you push with force and a set mind not to return void. Make sure you gain from your work with getting a plan to conquer. There are many ways to get your new book noticed and we will discuss this in the last chapter. Although you are determined to complete your book, once finished, you still need to push your new book. If you don't, do not expect anyone else too. It's time*

## Harmonize Your Purpose!

to introduce you to the world with branding your name.

This chapter, "Chasing After What Matter's," help identifies the author in you, cultivate your purpose and demonstrate a clear vision of whom you intend to be. "Chasing After What Matter's,' is from my book "The Birth of an Author Shall Be Born connects each to their divine assignments and help the vision write fulfills their visions. If you are writing an idea, a book, or starting a business? "The Birth of an Author Shall Be Born," is it you? Order today at www.pariceparker.biz

*Harmonize Your Purpose!*

# Chapter Four
## Let Your Heart Beat At Work

$O$ur last resource is always your best. The last shall be first, and the first shall be the last. Just when you think things are not going to happen, God will appear. God loves to take the least of all to get the job done right. Hebrews 11:3 says, "Through faith we understand that the worlds were framed by the word of God so that things which were seen were not made of things which do appear."

Many people have had the same opportunity as David, but they failed. Saul looked at Goliath and feared. He had all the Israelite's

## *Harmonize Your Purpose!*

standing with him in fear. No one in their human mind would stand up to this giant except David. Out of a whole army, He had the Faith that God would not let him die in this battle. Goliath was a known champion, and He had never defeated. We see things appearing before our eyes and some have caused us to fear the battle, but God wants you to move through your troubled state of mind. God does not want us ever to fear our situations, neither be afraid of going down in the valley. There is power in the valley, and you will receive it as you come out of it. David realized that the times he was in the valley; he gained greater power from God. Every trial has a wartime. One will be fighting against another. If you want your vision to speak, it is time to fight for it. Now it is your time, to step forward and face your giant.

### *Harmonize Your Purpose!*

*Show everyone around you that you have The Armies of God fighting for you. Often, we have to prove it to ourselves. It is time to pump up your belief and believe deeply in God that your visions are going to speak. Exercise your faith by remembering all the many challenges you have overcome with The Powers of God. This faith in God is going to cause you to say yes to His will and yes to His way. David continually reached for the heart of God. Regardless of his size, he depends on for God to be his help. God gave him the desires of his heart. He has been known to many Bible scholars to list in the hall of faith. Moreover, as many denounced, laughed, criticized and talked about David, God used the smallest one in the crowd with no skills of basic training to defeat Goliath. Imagine Saul as all the Israelite's were*

## *Harmonize Your Purpose!*

*standing with Him; none had the courage to go against Goliath. David was not old enough, he did not stand up to their statures, but David was ready to win this battle. However, in the eyesight of God, David was the perfect candidate to defeat the giant. God knew the size of David's faith. Remember; David was just the shepherd boy. He was only caught up in the midst because he was delivering food to the unit. Know that God is always in the midst. Though he was small, God fit all the power He needed in David to kill the giant. God loved the way David loved Him. He adored the way David believed in Him. David knew that God was the one that kept his heart beating through the works of his hands. Psalms 75:1 says, "Unto thee, O God, do we give thanks, unto thee do we give thanks: for that thy name is near thy*

### Harmonize Your Purpose!

wondrous works declare." God was the centerpiece of David's heart.

There must be a time to grow larger than self and the only way you can enlarge through The Anointing Powers of God. David had a repentant heart towards God; he was very conscientious about any mistakes that he had made. He never grew too large for God to be his supremacy. He never boasted in self because God obtained the glory. David made many mistakes in his lifetime. He was human just like you and me, but he kept trying to please God. David did not allow his sins or any mistakes stop him from attempting to satisfy his Living Go Psalms 51:10 says, "Create in me a clean heart, O God; and renew a right spirit within me."

## _Harmonize Your Purpose!_

_Though we have all made many mistakes, we should not let them stop us from trying to please God. Do not let those things keep you from winning your battle. Beating the enemy is God's full purpose for your life. God gains more as you win the victory. Beat the enemy with the good works of your hand. It's time you wash your hands of things that have held you back and of people that put stumbling blocks in your way. You will gain The Power of Righteousness. Everything in your life will begin to come together. God wants Excellency from us. At times, it seems as though things can never reach that manner but they can. Your hands are going to possess The Anointing Powers of God. However, they must stay prepared and ready to be used by Him at all times. Your heart is going to_

## *Harmonize Your Purpose!*

*drive your hands to the Anointing. And once your mind is made up in Him then you will do excellence in life. James 4:8 says, "Draw nigh to God, and he will draw nigh to you. Cleanse your hands, ye sinners; and purify your hearts, ye double minded."*

*If you take the opportunity to get closer to God, then surely it will make your vision speak sooner. I remember many years ago in my life, I went to church because of tradition. I never went on my free will or because I wanted to be there. Perhaps, I went because it was Sunday or I needed a blessing. These are the two reasons many people go to church. A vast majority only go when they need help. Going to church was not a priority for me. All those years I went in the*

## *Harmonize Your Purpose!*

*wrong state of mind. I could not tell you what the preached message was even before the altar calls, but I could tell you what the choir sang and how good it was. Through those years of my life, I stayed the same, and I had no power. Many times, we do not develop in the manner God wants us to because we are not trying to please Him. What is your life speaking today? Do you have a David Spirit or a Saul Spirit? God wants you to impress Him. Once you impress Him, then He will cause you to give others a better impression of living life with Him. Many will be inspired and impressed by you. Your spiritual leader is the one that feeds your life. David was fed through His faith and God continuously fed him power to be victorious. Be adequately through The Spirit of God and stay nourished. David truly knew God. Romans 10:17*

## *Harmonize Your Purpose!*

says, "So then faith cometh by hearing, and hearing by the word of God."

Some things that are causing conflict within your spiritual growth needs to cut out of your life. I do not believe that many people realize the many blessings that sin keeps many from attaining. It keeps many great things away from your life. If many could see what they miss out on, they would be sick. Love your freedom and love living life itself as God created you to live. Sin causes us to suffer more than one way. I have learned that it is not hard to cut sin out of your life, once you begin growing to a greater faith in God. Let your heart desire for the vision to enlarge your passion and cause you to be more prosperous. Anything that is crippling your faith

## *Harmonize Your Purpose!*

*or causing you from putting your hands on the powers of God let it or let them go. Get to know who He is. I was held captive for years, all because I did not understand His word. However, after I begin to get serious with my spiritual maturity, I grew in the word. It gave my life power. I do not mind offending sin by loving God greater. Sin has held me back long enough. I do not want to offend the God I so greatly love, need and appreciate in my life. Study the word for yourself, so that you can know the kind of God you serve. The Anointing releases you from bondage; it blesses as it covers your life and it brings forth peace. The Anointing gives you supernatural strength, and it will cause you to be a winner at all times. It destroys the yokes, and you will never have to carry another burden for the rest of your life. It*

### *Harmonize Your Purpose!*

will take care of you. Is sin worth The Anointing? Romans 10:17 says, "So then faith cometh by hearing, and hearing by the word of God."

The Anointing Powers of God will flow through your hands. Want to stay close to Him, know that cleanliness is next to Godliness. Lay your hands on the things that God would have you. I want my hands to be clean and pure for God so that He can operate His anointing on me. One day I received an emergency phone call, and God told me through my prayer life that I had an anointing in my hands. He said, "For anything to work that I must lay my hands on it." Now going to this hospital for this dying emergency I needed God right then and there. Often, people need God vessels to stay pure. Moreover, God requires us

## Harmonize Your Purpose!

every second of the day to be prepared to use Him. If we are not clean, our prayers may not be answered as we need them to be. I received an emergency call, and only The Anointing could heal this child. Imagine if I would have been living a double-minded life, waddling in sin. Perhaps, The Anointing would not have been able to work with me in prayer for this child. On the other hand, what if I did not know the word of God, I would not have trusted Him myself. There is more power than you realize in the word of God.

John 1:1 says, "In the beginning was the word, and the word was with God, and the Word was God." The Word gave me a purpose and a reason to stand, just as David. In any emergency,

### *Harmonize Your Purpose!*

*you need The Anointing ASAP. I needed the Armies of The Living God to ride with me, walk with me and to fight for this child's healing immediately. I prayed for this precious child. This child was in intensive care not expecting to make it, and the family needed God right then and there. This emergency required The Holy Spirit immediately. I felt the power of God flow through this request to heal this child. I am a firm believer in prayer power because it is the Holy Communion between God and His ordained vessels. If I were full of sin, then probably God would not have used me. However, that child needed The Anointing immediately to work powerfully in healing her body. It took every day of the last six years of my life to reach this kind of Anointing with God. I refuse to allow a sinful*

## *Harmonize Your Purpose!*

*nature to come and destroy The Anointing that God has bestowed upon my life. I refuse to let a little measly three-letter word such as sin, control any blessings that God wants in my life. Also, I refuse to jeopardize my eternal Glory to walk on the streets of Gold and destroy my eternal life. Now you can either seek God first at everything in your life or perhaps you can keep letting The Anointing just pass you buy. Do not allow a sin to control, guide, lead or the enemy to prepare your future. God deserves that Glory just gives your heart to Him daily. Mark 7:5 says, "Then the Pharisees and Scribes asked him, why to walk not thy disciples according to the tradition of the elders but eat bread with unwashed hands?" One day God enlightened my heart. I just knew that I needed the word. Then I begin applying every*

## *Harmonize Your Purpose!*

*word that I started receiving to my personal life because if one receives the word, then it needs heart application. No one can grow larger in the word without it being a heart application. If you do not have self-control, then the Word of God will teach you discipline. It will cause your heart to desire after righteousness. You will not be able to live in the same manner you used to. You will change for the better, and you will not be the same. Your ears will not want to hear the things they use to. Your legs will not wish to walk in the places they used to go. Your eyes will not look upon the things in the manner they used too. Also, you will have a change of heart on many things in your life. Your life will have a purpose to love God as you will desire to please Him. I am a firm believer that many people go to church in*

## *Harmonize Your Purpose!*

*such a familiar way (traditional). Nevertheless, many of people have forgotten to seek the way that God wants us to worship Him. I cannot seem to praise God as my mother did because I had to find my praise. I cannot clap my hands like my aunt because I had to feel the power of The Anointing clap through my hands. We cannot look to our forefathers and the way they worshiped God, for we must find Him for ourselves. You must worship Him in The Spirit and then God will teach you how Remember, the Spirit knows the Spirit by the Spirit and God Almighty is a spirit. John 4:23 says, "God is a Spirit: and they that worship him must worship him in spirit and truth." No matter how righteous we grow in the word, there is a need for continual washing of your hands before eating the bread of life. You*

## *Harmonize Your Purpose!*

*want to be pure and ready for God. Go to church with a mind prepared to receive Him. Get involved with the service and be inspired by the word. Treat the Word of God as your daily food, and it will feed you new life. It will nourish your soul and lift your spirit. The Word will cause you to run when you want to quit. It will fill your heart with inspirations and keep you working on your vision. It will feed you hope in a hopeless situation. Also, it will strengthen you where you are weak. The Word of God will bond you with The Anointing. Romans 10:17 says, "So then faith cometh by hearing, and hearing by the word of God."*

*I had to find my way to God by the putting on of my hands. I had to open up the word of God*

## *Harmonize Your Purpose!*

*for myself. Lay aside the things that will cause you to reject your personal faith growth. Research things on your own to grow spiritually. Many things I had to leave behind. I could not serve God as my parents did. I had to find my way with the reaching forth of my praise and with my hands. I am not a firm believer in many ordinary things because I never wanted to make tradition a God in my life. I believe in the God that I serve. He is so powerful, loving and caring. He will nurture your soul with righteousness. Know that He takes excellent care of your needs. God wants you to reach high for Him with the putting on of your hands. He will show you the way to The Truth and The Light. Let Him shine through you. Ecclesiastes 9:10 says, "Whatsoever thy hand findeth to do, do it with thy might; for there is no*

## *Harmonize Your Purpose!*

*work, nor device, nor knowledge, nor wisdom, in the grave, whither thou goest."*

*The only thing that is keeping your hands from working is you. It is up to you, and it will only achieve the measure of your faith. I am going to work with my hands as long as I have the strength of God in them. Want the works of your hands to achieve in the might of God. Nothing should stop you from receiving The Anointing. Do you want your life to be just a dream or you can begin reaching to obtain it. Let your vision be set free. You need your hands to work towards this vision and your fingertips to grasp this moment of hope? God would not have given them to you. Just think of your index finger and everything it is willing to point out to you*

## *Harmonize Your Purpose!*

*through the power of God. However, remember as you grab, just place it within the centerfold of your hands and begin to notice God as He will work with you. Hold on to the promise that God has given you because it is all in the palm of your hands. The more you begin to use what God has given you, the more you will be able to see Him work through you. Also, as you start to work this particular thing just watch how God will begin to anoint the works of your hands. God wants to keep your hands clean so He can bestow greater power beyond your imagination through the work of your hands. God wants us to use our hands not of our might but through His might. Work through His might and see that it has already had done. You must believe in the powers of God. Jesus did, and He received all power in His hands.*

## <u>Harmonize Your Purpose!</u>

*He worked His Heavenly Faith. Let your faith work for you; it will take you as high as you believe. Your faith will pull you out of every valley that you enter. It will cause you to win every battle, and you will be more than a conqueror. Faith has no limits.*

*Understand that through your might you are inspiring hope and through hope is your power. It will increase your faith possibility. Every time you think of the works of your hands does not look at the work of your hands as impossible. Look at the potential if you use them correctly. Your hands have the strength that you need to exercise daily. The vision that God has embedded in your mind use your hands to work it. Habakkuk 2:3 says, "For the vision is yet for an*

## *Harmonize Your Purpose!*

*appointed time, but at the end it shall speak, and not lie: though it tarries, wait for it: because it will surely come, it will not tarry." The Anointing will bring you out of all that you are going through, just use your hands.*

*Often, people that are striving for something strive too hard of themselves and not enough in God. Striving for self will destroy your vision but working with The Anointing will bring it to pass. Surely, God wants us to attempt but not in our might. God simply wants us to believe in Him and through Him that it is possible. God wants us to live life in abundance. For many of years, I tried by my might, and I continued to fall. I realize that all the visions God had given to me were through His ability. I struggled to strive. I*

### *Harmonize Your Purpose!*

*analyzed every possibility, and I kept coming up with remarkable ideas. Nothing seemed to be working out. I had to learn patience. James 1:3 says, "Knowing this, that the trying of your faith worketh patience." No, we do not like to wait, especially when we want things to happen right now. However, I learned to be patient with God. As God gives us vision, He will then provide us with a plan. Only through His power shall the plan be developed. Remember when God gives you idea it is greater than you. So, therefore, you will need His assurance for protection of your vision. God does not intend for us to overwork ourselves until we are purely exhausted. He intends for us to rely on Him. He loves being God so therefore let Him be the God over your vision. Let Him work His anointing powers through your hands.*

## _Harmonize Your Purpose!_

God is going to astonish you as you see it develop in your eyes. This work is going to simplify many things in your life and bring closure to your Giants. John 13:3 says, "Jesus knowing that the Father had given all things into his hands and that he has come from God, and went to God."

All of the works that Jesus accomplished came by The Anointing that worked through Him. Jesus had sought the direction, approval, and guidance power from JEHOVAH before He made a move. Heaven was His strength as He earnestly prayed. Regardless of what accomplishment, Jesus did it all to glorify His Father. Jesus intended His Father to strengthen Him in everything leaving Him out of nothing. We too must appear to God in the same manner as

## *Harmonize Your Purpose!*

*Jesus, reverencing Him. He needs to be in full control over everything in your life. Your prayer is your strength, and you can accomplish nothing perfectly out of this life without God's full gratitude and permission. If God is in it and if God gave you the vision then surely God is going to be your help. Jesus prayed tremendously unto His Father. He did not stop until God spoke to Him. Often we pray, but we do not give God the opportunity to talk back to us. Many say it does not take all day to pray, but it may take a while for God to speak back to you. I do not believe in putting a time limit on my prayer, neither do I like to rush my prayer. It is just as if you are rushing someone out the door because you have something else to do. We should not allow anything to hinder our prayer life nor to rush our*

### _Harmonize Your Purpose!_

*communion with God. Sometimes, God takes His time to listen and then He speaks to us. Kneel down with an expectancy to finish hearing from the Lord before you prepare to get up off your knees. Just imagine if Jesus would have gotten up too early off His knees as He talked to God? He would not possess all powers today. He would not have given God the opportunity to instill heavenly power inside him. Think about how much we leave at the prayer table all because we did not take the time to listen to God and rushed as we prayed. Mark 14:38 says, Watch ye and pray, lest ye enter into temptation. The Spirit truly is ready, but the flesh is weak.*

*Jesus knew that His life was only because of His Father's powers and so. Therefore, He*

## *Harmonize Your Purpose!*

*never had to analyze, think about or wonder when and if He needed to pray. Everyone in this world needs The Power of Prayer to make it through. Just as you and I, Jesus had to overcome many things. He suffered tremendously. People went to Him, and He too had a mission. It was to save you and me. All because of your vision, many will be encouraged. Jesus was very attentive unto His Father through prayer. Jesus needed Heavenly Powers to conquer the world, and God gave them to Him. He will also give you the power to conquer. Every work was because His Father led him first, guided Him through and gave Him the power to achieve. He listened to Heaven as He prayed. Many have asked the question, "How do you know when God is speaking to you." It cannot emphasize, for every individual hears Him*

## *Harmonize Your Purpose!*

*in a different manner. However, you will know His voice. Once you believe that your prayers have reached heaven, then He will speak plainly to you. You will hear Him as you will begin to follow Him. As you kneel, be prepared to listen to what God has to say to you. John 10:27 says, "My sheep hear my voice, and I know them, and they follow me:" Your prayer life is of your free will. The power that God will bestow in your life is up to how much power you are going to need in a lifetime. Jesus made sure He received all the power He would ever need. He continuously knelt down in prayer, and God continually gave Him power. I needed the strength of God to help me stand against the wiles of the devil. I also needed the power of God to help me continue in ministry. I could not walk as a minister in my ability for I*

## *Harmonize Your Purpose!*

*needed heavenly powers to help me. My ability is nothing if God is not the author of it. I cannot defeat the enemy without the Spirit of God. The enemy will choke you down if you do not have heavenly power. Hebrew 12:2 says, "Looking unto Jesus the author and finisher of our faith; who for the joy that was set before him endured the cross, despising the shame, and is set down at the right hand of the throne of God." He wants your hands to strengthen you with prayer power for the work completed. God wants you to seek His face and pay close attention to Him for He speaks power into your soul. As you prepared for your new prayer life? Be ready to receive greater powers from heavenly places. They will inspire your spiritual growth, as well as others that are around you. God is prepared to give you divine powers*

## *Harmonize Your Purpose!*

*that you never knew. Be ready to do the wondrous works by the putting on of your hands with the anointing power of God. He is a God of action, and as you begin your new prayer life, God is going to act on your prayers. Just remember never to stop praying for it quenches your spiritual growth. Continue to pray every day as though you are praying for the last time. From this day forward, you will become more powerful. Know that God moves as we pray and He listens as we speak to Him. Heaven will hear you as it will open the doors of blessings to cover your life. Jesus knew the many secrets of God, and He received His powers. Get to know the secrets of God and be empowered. This chapter "Let Your Heart Beat at Work," is from my book "The Anointing Powers of Your Hands." A book that causes individuals to*

### *Harmonize Your Purpose!*

*plow forcefully. There is so much power produced in the works of the hand and it's the real mission of bringing forth evidence. If you want greater substance, inhabit a more concrete faith and to be more fruitful then order The Anointing Powers of Your Hands today! www.pariceparker.biz*

*Harmonize Your Purpose!*

# Chapter Five
*Your Destiny is In Your Purpose*

*T*he key to unlocking your destiny is useful pushing purpose? I have claimed some beautiful and expensive things in my lifetime. More than an average income could supply. Only my faith could deliver me, so, therefore, I realized I had to utilize my gifts. Your destiny is in your purpose, and your heart will lead you to your destiny. If, you follow your heart. Psalm 84:11 says, For the Lord God is a sun and shield: the Lord will give grace and glory: no good thing will he withhold from them that walk uprightly. Keep your promises in your sight, never letting them go. The Lord rewards those that deserve it. Know

## Harmonize Your Purpose!

that you are doing something that deserves awards, and then expect your prize. Occasionally, go by and put claims on things that you can't afford, but that your heart desires. Touch some things that are tasteful and useful, want them with a passion. Post them in your eyesight. Just stay reminded of everything that God said He was going to do for you. God spoke to me when I was going through, and I could not see my way out. My eyes saw darkness, but my heart felt the light. My bank account was negative, but God told me I was rich. I claimed things that my money could not buy in a 10-year life span, but God told me you are going to be able to pay cash for it. He is a God of His word and His word is true. Make sure you keep your purpose in your eyesight. It is just like a child wanting candy, and as long as they

## *Harmonize Your Purpose!*

*can crave the sweetness, they will do what you tell them to do to get it. Post it up on your mirror, in your kitchen, office or perhaps on your car dashboard- just keep it in your sight. As long as you can keep your eyes on the prize, then you will run and not get tired. You will recognize the power that is in your gift(s). Your faith will grow because you will be able to keep your hope alive. Keep your visions in your sight, hold on to them. Post it where you can see it every day. Allow your goals to be seen by your eyes and think of your result. Stand on it and don't be moved, no matter how hard times get; just hold on to your prize as if you have already won it. When you hold onto it in that manner, then you will finish what you have started. If you hold onto it as if you already have it, then you are walking through the finish line*

### *Harmonize Your Purpose!*

with your arms up. God Is Waiting On You At The Finish Line. Ecclesiastes 9:11 says, I returned, and saw under the sun, that the race is not to the swift, nor the battle to the strong, neither yet bread to the wise, nor yet riches to men of understanding, nor yet favor to men of skill; but time and chance happened to them all. God wants you to know that He is waiting for you at the finish line, and He wants His praise even before you complete this task. It's your chance to get it right, so, that He can bless you righteously. He is trying to give you – your heart's desires. He has your new life waiting at the finish line. He is rooting for you to run on. Your hope for tomorrow is in every forward step that you make right now. The harder you run, the more hope you'll gain. Your joy unspeakable is at the finish

## *Harmonize Your Purpose!*

line of this journey. If you could ask Isaiah, Job, and Abraham how did they make it – surely they will tell you it wasn't easy. God is sure that they will tell you to keep moving forward, hold onto your faith and through it all just trust God. They kept stepping forth, and they did not let anything stop them. Though times they may have tarried, and times they may have come to a halt, but they never stopped taking their steps forward. Though sin sometimes may have gotten them off the right track, it was the love of God that routed them to their finish line. Though the road was hard, and sometimes they got discouraging, they kept on moving anyhow. They kept their eyes prepared and ready to see the finish line of faith. Your prosperity is at the finish line, your wealth, and all your promises are waiting for you at the finish

## *Harmonize Your Purpose!*

*line. All those things that you have ever imagined good to happen in your life are at the end of your finish line - along with every heart drenching prayer. By the way, the more laps you run the sooner you will get to the finish line. The more effort you put in the works of your hands, the sooner you will be rewarded. Regardless of your skills, God can use them for His glory. He wants you to take what you have and run with it. No matter how fit you are for this journey; continue to allow Gods Anointing Power to get you in perfect shape. That idea and dream; that gift is all yours because God gave it to you. Now, move with it, step in it and live it to the fullness, because God's Anointing Power is in it. He wants your hands on it so that you can live your acceptable year of the Lord. Isaiah 61:2 says, To*

## _Harmonize Your Purpose!_

*proclaim the acceptable year of the Lord, and vengeance of our God; to comfort all that mourn. Now God is transforming all of your nothings into something. He is bringing forth the evidence that He has heard your cry. All those long nights that you yielded your heart unto Him, you poured out from your belly the hell that has tormented you. Also, all those enemies that stole your possessions took the things you love for a selfish gain. They tried to destroy you. Romans 12:14 says, Bless them which persecute you: bless and not curse. As He visits your enemies, He will let them know who you are in Him. He will cause them to have to come unto you with blessings and good deeds seeking forgiveness. God will restore everything that was taken out of your life, as He restores you. You will be more blessed with bigger*

### *Harmonize Your Purpose!*

*and better. It is your Hallelujah time because the victory is now yours. All that mourned when you mourned, prayed and cried along by your side will receive the overflow of your blessings. They too will be restored. Oh, now He is straightening out some crooked stuff within your enemies that caused you to cry, and that upset you. It is just as a child that got beat up by that neighborhood bully and ran home to tell their daddy, boy a daddy wouldn't let anyone beat up their child, and get away with it. That daddy is going to be like a wolf. He's going to straighten out the bully, and as they see the dad coming down the street, they are going to know that trouble is on its way. Immediately, they will begin to fear. So don't worry about your enemies. God will have all vengeance against every enemy that has ever come*

## *Harmonize Your Purpose!*

*up against you. Because when they come against you, they messed around with a child of God. That is why Satan is sitting in hell right now because He messed around with God. The enemy forgot that Jesus has the keys to hell and guess what, He is your vindicator. Just as long as you are in God, and He is in you, and then you too possess those same keys to hell. I mean every part of it, so do not worry. Romans 12:19 says, Dearly beloved, avenge not yourselves, but rather give place unto wrath: for it is written, vengeance is mine; I will repay, saith the Lord. Just keep in mind that God did it all for you. He remembered every heavy load, every burden that you carried and every weight that you lifted while you were trying all that you had. Just because many hurt you as you tried, God does not ever want you to turn out to*

## *Harmonize Your Purpose!*

*be another one of them. He wants you always to walk in love, kindness and to do many good deeds as a righteous warrior that has won the battle. God is going to turn your entire life around. The work of your hands is going to prove to many that the Hands of The Lord Is upon You. It will be noticeable to all to see that God is in you. So, therefore, continue to represent in Love. Represent in a right manner, be a real God ambassador. Romans 12:21 says, Be not overcome by evil, but overcome evil with good. For every time that you were confused, and you brought to shame, God is going to grant you a double to a hundred-fold return. Your reward will be your inheritance; it calculated for your portion of faith. If you grow large in faith, then your part will be great. If you only have a little faith, then your inheritance part*

## *Harmonize Your Purpose!*

will be small. However, if your faith has no limits on how much God can bless you, then your legacy will never stop calculating. Once you finish here on this earth, absolutely no one will be able to count your value. Remember what He had told you. Well, now it is at an all-time high; just as if the stock market has hit the top of the roof and your increase breaks through. God is going to grant you more than you can imagine for all your troubles. Your acceptable year is the year that God will find and bestow the favor of increase upon you. Every stronghold that binds you; through every locked down and imprisoned situation, God said, "It's your FREEDOM TIME." Heaven is about to release every promise that God promised you, just because you held out and held on. God is unlocking every locked up blessing that kept you

## *Harmonize Your Purpose!*

*from prospering. You know all those dreams that you have had and God brought forth a new covenant, well it is pay-day time, payback time and over-pay time. Your gain is going to be larger than your eyes could ever see. Why, because you trusted the Lord to be your help. When everyone belittled you, laughed at you and scandalized you – you held on. Why, because you have been crazy enough to believe in all these crazy dreams that God was going to do this thing for you. So, therefore, God is going to give you every desire of your heart; including the desires that you have forgotten. Isaiah 61:8 says, For I the LORD love judgment, I hate robbery for burnt offering; and I will direct their work in truth, and I will make an everlasting covenant with them. Now you know that God has anointed your hands for this job*

## *Harmonize Your Purpose!*

*because it is now fruitful and multiplying if it have not yet then it will. Only God can cause such an enrichment of prosperity and joy to come into your life. God loves satisfying with the truth that is why the truth shall set you free. As one of my good friend's mother always says, "Baby one thing God loves, it isn't anything but the truth, and I tell you that's what He loves." His Anointing Powers has the key that is going to cause those closed doors to open as you begin to walk towards them. When the tree of David had been cut down, the stump still had life in it. Though many things seemed to try to cut down the works of your hands, it still has a life form. God owns the root, and your power source is the owner of heaven, with all rights to produce any miracle that you will ever need. Also, as long as*

## *Harmonize Your Purpose!*

*God is the root, then why are you worried? It is going to grow; you do not have to water it because God is going to water it with His increase. Just as the seeds are sown, your ground has already begun the tilling process, and seed cannot sit but so long. After your seed takes ground root, no matter what seed you sewed, it shall spring forth. Notice as the buds sprout their way out of the ground it will burst forth and then burst through. Now, you won't be able to see that day as it broke through the ground. You may look one day and still see no bud coming forth, but if you look again, you'll see the bud sitting right there. It snuck its way through while you weren't looking. Everything that you have sowed through your effort, through your will power, through your determination, and through your diligent work -*

## *Harmonize Your Purpose!*

*God will direct an order per seed you have sown. All seeds must burst through; all seeds have time to grow so be patient as your seeds grow. God wants you to have all new fruit in your life. The Anointing Powers that are in Your Hands are going to produce new fruit in your life. Are you ready?*

*Most people look for the judgment as a bad thing, but from God fearing believers we shall receive a righteous reward. God will judge you for everything that you did right. He will set an everlasting promise with you that will be made according to what He decides you deserve. I believe God for the covenant that He has made in my life. I want my promises and the land it sets on to flow with milk and honey. God's promises*

## *Harmonize Your Purpose!*

*are true. God loves to be satisfied with good works, and as you please God with the Works of Your Hands, He will allow you more favor. He will fulfill His promises to you. The more you satisfy Him, the more power you will receive; He will give you larger works to do. God is a God of increase, a God of faithfulness and a God that will establish excellent works. As you prove to Him that you are faithful in your divine assignment, He will fulfill your vision to be large. He will grant you every real reward because He has accepted your work with gladness in His heart. It is a beautiful thing when we satisfy God because He fulfills our every need and He will not rest until He accurately meets you. Isaiah 61:11 says, For as the earth bringeth forth her bud, and as the garden causeth the things that are sown in it to*

## *Harmonize Your Purpose!*

*spring forth; so the Lord GOD will cause righteousness and praise to spring forth before all the nations.*

*I pray that this book has brought you to your "ACCEPTABLE YEAR OF THE LORD" and that it has been more than you ever expected it to be in your life. In this is the year to expect things you've only dreamed of to appear in your life. It is valuable that you work with the Anointing Powers that God has given you. Utilize your gifts and keep them covered. There are many accomplishments by the works of your hands and the vision(s) that God has assigned unto you. I believe in The Anointing Powers of God and that no hands can accomplish a greater work without The Anointing. Keep in mind that*

### *Harmonize Your Purpose!*

*every seed that you have sown, through your job ethic, effort, self-will, monetary, and so on that God is going to release your ground with the buds of all of your sown seeds. Some seeds you may have forgotten that you sowed and not all you can count. Just let God do the calculations while you send up your praises. Very soon it is all going to make men as well as you say; we serve an AWESOME GOD. The hands of the Lord are upon you, and the Anointing Powers Are in your Hands. Use them for His Glory and He shall bless your gift(s) as He shall receive greater glory. Praise Him for He is Worthy and Praise Him for all your buds springing forth fruit in your land of increase. Rejoice, because this is Your Acceptable Year of The Lord. Though many things in your life seemed to be empty, God is going to fulfill*

## *Harmonize Your Purpose!*

*them all. Yes, this is your year where you shall gain favorable increase, so rejoice and be glad. One night as I was talking to my aunt Pauline, we were discussing happiness. At that time, I had so many wrong things going on in my life, until I forgot all about being happy. I was trying hard to make everyone else happy until I forgot about myself. Through our conversation, she said, "Baby have you ever prayed for happiness." I thought for a minute, and I realized I wanted to be happy, but I never desired to be happy. It hit me from that day forward. As I thought more and more about happiness, I realized I thought of some things that would make me happy. My happiness was not in things because things can't love you back. You know sometimes we can believe that if God blesses us with something that we have*

### *Harmonize Your Purpose!*

*wanted, that it will make us happy. Well, that is not true. Because as soon as you get it, the newness will fade away and then you will find yourself starting over and over again wanting something else. I thought of many things that would make me happy, but it was the one thing that God had given me, that truly caused my happiness. This gift contains joy late in the midnight hour, more valuable than gold, the brightest light that will never dim, dominion with all power; nothing will ever top this gift. It is too useful to price, and not everyone can receive it though it is one of a kind. It is the largest, most beautiful and powerful gift you will ever receive, and He wants your appreciation. In this gift, there is power to conquer your beginning and end. Jesus is the light in your darkest hours, and life*

## _Harmonize Your Purpose!_

*for eternity. Though His gift took many years to develop, it's still growing today through our faith, as we grow stronger in the Lord. Know that Jesus paid the ultimate price. On the cross when He commended Himself to God, He Gave JEHOVAH all that He had and for that only JEHOVAH gave Him All Power. Jesus always showed great Honor towards His Heavenly Father. Just as Jesus rose up, you can too with your Precious Gift from God, through the Blood of Jesus the Christ. He is your Opportunity to the tree of Life. Utilize your gift, and use this opportunity to gain the greatest life you can. Excellent life opportunity is in using your gift so, therefore, take advantage of it. Be blessed, be a praiser and become a victorious warrior. Remember, whatever you desire, whatever you seek after is what you will find. So,*

### Harmonize Your Purpose!

therefore, seek after the heart of Jesus and watch how He will ultimately bless your life. Also, note, your destiny is packed in your gift, so unwrap it and show it to the world.

Wow, this chapter "Your Destiny Is In Your Purpose," AWE, it's IMACCULATE! It's from my book, "A Precious Gift from God," and it is your destiny connector! Your praise will never be the same after reading this book, and it will thrust you into our destiny. Order this book today, "A Precious Gift From God," www.pariceparker.biz

*Harmonize Your Purpose!*

# Chapter Six
*If I Can, You Can Relocate*

Yes, I walked out of everything I had after I heard the voice of the Lord say, "take only a duffel bag for your journey and my family packed a duffel bag a piece. We left Charlotte, and things grew only worse before getting better. I came back to Georgia. I heard the voice of the Lord. He said, "Go Back to Georgia there is a GREAT and Work Unfinished you must complete!" I told my husband what the Lord said, and he nodded his head yes. I said, "not to sell anything just open the doors and give it away." Oh, when the word got out that is all it took. I only put a few things in storage such as important papers, pictures, and

### Harmonize Your Purpose!

keepsake items. Afterward, we begin our new journey to Georgia with seven bucks and a quarter tank of gas. We left Charlotte. Once I came back to Charlotte, it was the hardest year I ever had and the unhappiest I have ever experienced. All along I was missing Georgia, but I also remember my previous struggles there. It is extremely hard when God expect so much of a person. I felt I was entirely alone, and nothing was filling my void. Trying to make a long story short but my old friend girl use to say, "you make a long story long! Lol.

For years here and there I heard your voice telling me,"I want you to publish my book." And, I thought I had lost your book. All encouraging words give visionaries a reason to push especially those that go through extreme life experiences.

## <u>Harmonize Your Purpose!</u>

*See, after I moved back to Georgia in 2011, I did not know where I was going to live. Nevertheless, I just got on the road because I figured since I heard the voice of the Lord that He would also open doors. All I had to my name was seven bucks and a quarter tank of gas before I begin my journey. So once we saw the sign welcome to Georgia. I then called my husbands niece. She was the one that did not want me to leave Georgia before, but I did. Now, we were passing the sign, and my heart begins to rush. In my mind I thought, "What was I thinking to give everything away and where are my children and my family going to live"? My daughter was in college, and she sacrificed her jeep so we could have transportation. It was one of the scariest moments in my life, not knowing where we were going to*

## Harmonize Your Purpose!

*live but I had no choice. I know I heard His voice. Do I begin to dial his niece phone number not knowing what she would say? She answered, "Hello?" I told her I gave up everything, and we had just passed the Georgia state line. We did not have anywhere to live, and I asked her, "could we sleep on your floor until I get back on my feet?" She said, "come on." I told her, "it won't be long at all just likely a few weeks." A great, relief came over me because I have never followed the voice of the Lord that extreme.*

*So as time goes by daily my husband and I got up working and treading the ground with my CD "Somebody Say, Jesus." God deleted all my resources, finances and old ways of survival. He made me aggressive because I was too passive. On the streets of Georgia God gave me a better insight*

## _Harmonize Your Purpose!_

on how to run my vision such as Fountain of Life Publisher's House. In our past experiences of you getting to know me, I was not near as prepared to publish other author's as I am now. He was not complete with directing my steps, vision directions and giving me strategy points to publish other authors. As I continued building a new life, a new vision and gaining a new strength, The Holy Spirit trained me directly.

The reason I thought I had lost your book is because one day. I received a called from our storage unit, and if I, did not submit payment, I would lose my storage unit. I was struggling, and could only pay the storage or paid the church hotel bill. I decided to pay the hotel for church so we can worship Sunday. Once I made that decision, I went into the bathroom and shut the door. I looked

### <u>Harmonize Your Purpose!</u>

in the mirror, and I cried. All of my relevant paperwork, family portraits, and some keepsake items was in the storage. All the rest we had given away. As I cried, I asked Jesus "whoever you let buy my storage room, please let them have the heart of Jesus, and give me my children pictures back. Lord, I have suffered enough, please stop allowing me to prosecutions, I don't deserve it!"

*Harmonize Your Purpose!*

# Chapter Seven
## Be Persistent

Systematically, to obtain your heart's desires, you must get persistent with your wants! Your faith must be activated. Overcoming is a spiritual system, and not everyone can tolerate their test. The only way is to The Almighty. You must grasp it with a pure heart determination until you seize what yours is. When you face the facts, and realize that enough is enough. You will begin to move forward with a perseverance that nothing or no one will get in your way. Enough is enough. You must make things happen, and be determined to conquer. Be a go getter and not a go-sitter. It will not matter what do not have; you

## *Harmonize Your Purpose!*

*will simply know that enough is enough. You will not be able to take another devastation in your life. You will, by all means necessary, do everything that is in your power to push your faith to move. No longer will you consider what you need to make it because now you will be operating through The Supernatural. Simply saying, "It is now out of my hands, Jesus it is in yours." Regardless of what you need, you will begin to make things work. Your vision and ideas will become a rare moment, and nothing will stop your vision. Not even need! You will figure out a way when you can't take one more thing! Know that enough is enough. Believe all things are possible through Christ. Take control of every aspect of your life, by gaining intelligence through the WORD. Adopt the WORD of faith every day in*

## *Harmonize Your Purpose!*

*your life and let it push you to fortune. Philippians 4:6, "Be careful for nothing; but in everything by prayer and supplication with thanksgiving let your requests be made known unto God." Job 6:8, "Oh that I might have my request; and that God would grant me the thing that I longed for!" Take your request to God. Be prepared to embrace every word that He has given you. Make it happen through gaining access to Heavenly Powers. When you begin to grasp the visual aspects of your request, then you will receive favor from on high. (11 Corinthians 2:9) God's favor will make everything in your life come together, and totally line up with the word. It will create fruitfulness to overwhelm your life. This is the time; you must grasp the true hope of security. Always abide in HIM and Hold on to*

## *Harmonize Your Purpose!*

*your faith. Your faith is what gets your request to The Almighty. Your faith is what gives you power. It will deliver any that are in need and speak life to the walking dead. Faith will allow you to move from one place to another. Your heart will lead you to the truth and no longer just a dream surrounded by clouds. When you give no attention to your assailants that have tried to assault your mind, then you will not feel the irritations of aggravations, that is when you think bad things are happening to you in your life. It will seem to bring more trouble. Instead of focusing on the worst, hold on to good. I always like to find one good reason or purpose out of every bad situation instead of letting thing during my eviction; I could not give into the problem of my eviction. I immediately gave The Almighty the*

## Harmonize Your Purpose!

*praise for a brand new house. No matter what I felt, God had covered my steps and ordered them. Though one door in my life closed, I knew, without a shadow of a doubt, that God was giving me the keys to my new home. I praised Him for a better home and received one. It was bigger and better than what I previously had. God is getting ready to bless you with bigger and better, just be patient.*

*Job 31:15, "Did not he that made me in the womb make him? and did not one fashion us in the womb?" So now is the time for you to stand stronger and in bigger faith in The Almighty. Quite naturally, if he did it for Job then he too will do the same for you. You must believe that The Almighty wants to give you bigger and better things that this world cannot offer you. He will*

## *Harmonize Your Purpose!*

*give you things that money cannot buy and things not made by mans' hands. No matter what your eyes currently see, know that The Almighty is still in control. We search for many man-made reasons as to why this thing is happening. Still, no real answer. We are purposed to look for the unsearchable riches of our Heavenly Father. Put all your trust in The Almighty as Job did, that is why he received so much. He knew The Almighty had all power; he knew God was still in charge of his life. Job realized that no matter what. He was covered by the Word of God and Job previously knew many that couldn't hold on, as they suffered. Job knew the consequences of not being patient. He also knew he could not do it by himself. It was only after the request he made to his Heavenly Father. Afterward, he was made*

## *Harmonize Your Purpose!*

*whole again. Although it did not come overnight, it took time. Job could not stop proving himself to The Almighty, just because some things rose up in his life. He was not prepared to allow anything to separate or come in-between him and The Most High. The ONE that has always been there for him. Job knew it was nobody, but the Almighty that had previously blessed him. He was not willing to trust another to be God over his life. He too realized that there were many gods, but only one that was his! I believe that is why he made sure to call on the right one. He did not want a pagan god coming to his rescue. One thing I realized on my spiritual journey is that often we can speak the wrong things to happen in our lives. If you have a complaining spirit, then you are making it your god. What if one has a lazy spirit,*

### *Harmonize Your Purpose!*

*they too may lack and doubt their God. God is a spirit, and we must get an understanding of The Most High. Once one believes in The Most High, complaints will be far away! Things in one's life will transform from bad to good. Words create gods because what you speak comes into existence. If one speaks negative or trouble, it comes. When one speaks life, things begin to uplift. Perhaps, your words are causing downers and doubts, or uppers are causing prosperity to form in your life. Be careful of the things that come out of your mouth, because it is creating your future! So believe in the Spirit of The Most High and watch how He will raise you up! So, therefore, one day I wondered as Job was becoming tired, whom did he call on? I found out - The Almighty! He is the one that has all might. At that time, Jesus had not*

## Harmonize Your Purpose!

been born. Then I also wondered who did Adam & Abraham call. It was I AM.   Exodus 3:13 & 14 When Moses questions God, who shall I said me and asked me your name. And God said unto Moses, "I AM THAT I AM, I AM hath sent me." Too many times people tend to describe The Most High and it's hard when I AM could be all things. I realized that I was not going to waste any more time in trying to figure all things out and begin working all things out in my life that is not producing. I AM everything that I am not. I AM everything I need. If I need a miracle healing, I AM is the HEALER. If I need a miraculous break through, I AM is the Master of BREAKTHROUGHS. If I need deliverance from anything, I AM is a DELIVERER. Whatever you need I AM is your need Supplier! He only

## Harmonize Your Purpose!

produces life in abundance! Speaking, I AM the master of your needs, wants and heart's desires! He is your master, and I AM works through your faith. No one could supply your need greater than JESUS. It is by your FAITH that you shall be made whole. Not a day sooner, not a day later but your vision shall speak. Once your faith activates you NOW, I AM will produce!

In my mother's womb, I AM fashioned, and my future destined with righteousness. Though I had to go through, it was all for the glory of I AM to be revealed. I have never noticed I AM to dress anyone to look a mess. You must believe everything that has occurred in your life, for the purpose of The Almighty to be evident through you. You are His walking evidence. In you is a wealthy inheritance and through your great

## *Harmonize Your Purpose!*

*substance shall be produced! When the devil wants to make you look a mess, show him what I AM can do. The Word strictly instructs us that if we seek The Kingdom of GOD (I AM) first, then all else will be added to our lives. It did not specify just a few things, but all things not excluding anything whatsoever. Only you have the ability to make your request known unto our Heavenly Father. Seek for The Kingdom of God (I AM). He will make all things happen for you and in your life. Diligently, seek Him because there is so much to learn of Him. We simply do not have time to rest on our journey; we must diligently seek Him. Proverbs 10:4, "He becometh poor that dealeth with a slack hand: but the hand of the diligent maketh rich." You are a wealth representative, and your life is speaking for The Kingdom.*

## *Harmonize Your Purpose!*

*Imagine your children in the store looking a hot mess with dirty shoes and dirty clothes. Someone may ask, "Where are your parents?" they point their finger at you. Noticing you look well dressed, how would it make you feel? Would it make you feel good about how they represent you? No. What would they see, when they catch you in a mess? Many in the Bible that overcame were more than conquers. As you seek Him, He will cause you to discover mysteries of how to be blessed in abundance. He wants to show others the adequate rewards of Kingdom mind setters! The more I seek for Him, the more I am taught of Him. Proverbs 8:17, "I love them that love me; and those that seek me early shall find me." The sooner you find Him, the sooner your request will be made known. He is the only one with all your*

## *Harmonize Your Purpose!*

*needs. He has everything your heart ever desired, and He wants to give it to you. It is simple if you seek Him first. Seek His approval in everything you do and you will be righteously rewarded. God grants us privileges, blessings, power, and access through our faithfulness. Let Him add great things to your life. Then the scripture clearly states that He will add all things unto you. Being obedient only subjects the power of The Almighty to be given unto you. He will be responsible for you. Remember Matthew 6:33 "but seek ye first the kingdom of GOD, and His righteousness and all these things shall be added unto you." Once you realize the importance of giving The Almighty your undivided attention, your mind will remain in Him and His Word. He will begin to create things that you never thought were*

## *Harmonize Your Purpose!*

*possible, from material to Wisdom. So many believers cause their aggravations. They ask The Almighty for a special request, but they quit seeking Him on their journey towards it. Also, some cannot handle how he delivers it to them. The same way you gain is the same spiritual strategy you must keep obtaining. Just keep putting Him first. II Corinthians 1:9, "But we had the sentence of death in ourselves, that we should not trust in ourselves but in God, which raiseth the dead:"*

*What if Job would have begun to trust himself, vice versa the Word of the Almighty. He would have never made it out alive. Often we lose ourselves during the struggles of life. Continue seeking after righteousness, do not trust anything or any other God. I once knew this person as they*

## *Harmonize Your Purpose!*

begin to trust their friends. The more they stop feeding themselves righteousness, the more Satan enjoyed himself in their life. This person was brutally attacked. This person was getting beat so bad until they hardly fought back. I tried to help, but they did not want to receive it. As I looked at the individual, I began to pray more. I start to run faster to safety. I also kept the Word growing in my life, by keeping it nearer. The worst thing in life is when you cannot hear The Almighty. I felt for this individual, because as I saw them critically suffer. I said, "All they need is to call on JESUS!" In most cases, many make their situation worse, because they stop putting God first. There is absolutely no greater trust on the face of this earth to invest in, other than The Almighty. Jesus is the way maker, and He is

## *Harmonize Your Purpose!*

*powerful. (Matthew 28:18, "And Jesus came and spake unto them, saying, All power is given unto me in heaven and earth.") No matter what you need, He will go and make the way so you can obtain it. If you do not ask, then how will you ever receive? Seeking is an action word, just like faith. It searches when you search, and it finds what it seeks. If you never take a decision on your request, then how can you truly receive it? Your faith will get you there, but faith without works are dead.*

*Job 31:2, "For what portion of God is there from above? and what inheritance of the Almighty from on high?" Sometimes you will look at others like you are in desperate need. Or perhaps, without the ability to carry on. Those same people that talked about you scandalized your name and*

## Harmonize Your Purpose!

tried to put your name to shame. One day The Almighty is going to use it all, for a token of His good. (Psalms 86:17) He will show others, who they went against. Also, those that were your enemies, The Almighty will make them be your footstool. During your faith-building process, be steadfast and unmovable. At all times, look through your spiritual eyes. You will make it. Job was determined to overcome. Through his sickness, his mind was made up. After all, he lost; his mind was made up to wait patiently on The Lord. Maybe, Job remembered how he was there for others during their time of need. One that blesses those that are less fortunate always has a higher power to look up. Psalms 41: 1, "Blessed is he that considereth the poor: the LORD will deliver him in time of troubles." Job believed in

## Harmonize Your Purpose!

the Almighty; He knew his portion of deliverance. Job blessed many people, and his life was dedicated to being a blessing. He was aware that The Almighty would protect him, during his times of need. Psalms 41:2, "The LORD will preserve him, and keep him alive; and he shall be blessed upon the earth: and thou wilt not deliver him unto the will of his enemies."

Sometimes as we go through tough times, many tend to appear blameless. Often I looked back over my life and many times, I could not understand why the enemy was assaulting me. My response, I too had not been what I needed to be. It could be something such as growing in patience; understanding faith has a mighty way of operating on you. The enemy in most cases wants us frustrated as to why we are being tried. Also,

## Harmonize Your Purpose!

we overlook something so simple and innocent. Such as patience being highly developed to formulate us to a particular faith. The one that pleases The Most High. Job had faith that ultimately pleased The Almighty and all that Job endured completed The Most High in him. Afterward, his faith possessed divine substance, double for his trouble!

As I spiritually matured I realized, it was not easy. Honestly, if it had not been for me holding on to The WORD. I would have lost my mind. If I had not knelt down to pray, I would have gone crazy. If I had not tuned into The Holy Spirit, I would have not survived. Job 31:6, "Let me be weighed in an even balance, that God may know my integrity." Though we must endure life assaults, we have to allow them to strengthen us

## *Harmonize Your Purpose!*

*in areas where we are weak. Integrity is when you hear the I AM in you and know that you must maintain a supernatural ability to be incorruptible. You must grow to a certain faith that nothing can intercept your spiritual manifestation. Being incorruptible is the integrity God requires of the ones that please Him. Regardless of what one is going through, he still will promote the KINGDOM, no matter what state your life is. The incorruptible always walk by faith, and they never see with their natural eyes. Once the pure faith is birthed through you, no one would ever be able to persuade you of another God. Neither would they be able to take you away from Jesus. Your life shall speak and persuade them, that He is at large in you. Sooner*

## Harmonize Your Purpose!

than later, they would have to inquire on whom you serve. You too can tell them, I AM!

I too thought I was strong enough in The Almighty until I begin to go through my greatest trial. It was life threatening. Job knew who he was beforehand. Afterward, I can imagine. WOW! The average person would have given up and rolled over as well as died. However, Job grew in patience because He knew what he was before he was finished! Wow! What an effect being patient will have in your life. Job 31:6, "Let me be weighed in an even balance, that God may know my integrity." After all Job went through he was evenly balanced. Perhaps, the same is happening to you. He is balancing out the fruit of His spirit in you. One thing I realized is that the Almighty wants us evenly balanced. As we are being

### *Harmonize Your Purpose!*

*developed with integrity, we must be evenly balanced. Not too much of this and in the need of that. Job was highly developed until his integrity was complete. Our Heavenly Father wants all the ruins to be removed out of our lives. Understand the way He is developing me may not be the way He causes you to be remade. Perhaps, the greatest key to this story is that when God was looking at Job, he was looking into His future once He finished him. When God puts His eyes on something, He can see the good and know the value. Probably, that could have been the reason God looked upon Job as pleasing unto His eyesight. However, He knew how perfect Job was going to come out once He finished developing Job's integrity. After all, his integrity began to show how much he valued The Most High. If you*

## Harmonize Your Purpose!

be loyal to Jesus, He must return the favor from The Most High to be loyal to you.

Job 21:6, "Even when I remember I am afraid, and trembling taketh hold on my flesh." When the strongholds of your life are stronger than you, then you need the immediate strength you have never known. You need the strength of a Shield to protect you from the fiery darts of life. You need a mountain Rock, to cover you when the forces of the enemy are roaring against you and the Oil of your Butter to give you sliding ability. A King that can give you perfect direction, lead you out of the pattern of destruction; also, a Shepherd to look after you when you are headed in harm's way. He is a Judge that will correct you when you are inconceivably wrong; a Refuge that will fight your battle during the times you give up. He has a

## *Harmonize Your Purpose!*

*Fortress of power that you can gain victorious strength, of the highest capacity. An Avenger to avenge your death in the case of a wounded heart and He has the power to demolish any weapon that has formed against you. Our Heavenly Father is a Creator that can speak anything into existence. Miraculous Healer - when the doctors tell you there is nothing that they can do, because He is the Savior of all the earth. A Protector from all hurt, harm, danger, and evil. He is a Provider of sufficiency so that every need in your life will be bountifully met and met on time. A Redeemer to awaken any dead thing within you, so that your soul will be granted the Eternal Life promised with pure happiness and peace. He is my Prince of Peace. He is Mercy forever more and full of Grace. Also, Jesus is the truth, always*

## Harmonize Your Purpose!

showing me the way towards His marvelous Light.

This chapter "Be Persistent," is from my book "Aggravated Assault On Your Mind." When you recognize, enough is enough, and you cannot tolerate one more thing. Be a go getter and not a go-sitter. It will not matter what do not have; you will simply know that enough is enough. "Aggravated Assault On Your Mind," is the original seed "Book" of Fountain of Life Publisher's and al that orders "Aggravated Assault On Your Mind," plus ready it shall inherit a Fountain of Life! Order your copy today www.paricparker.biz

*Harmonize Your Purpose!*

# Chapter Eight
*Run Conqueror Run*

Your spiritual trainer matters. You have to know how to use what you have. If something is working incorrectly, then there is a problem. It is alright to clarify something to obtain the right information. To push whatever is in you out. You must have pushing power because if you don't you will be in plenty of pain. There is only one way to stop the birthing pains of your vision; you must push until it comes out. Quiet noticeably the pains come again because simply what's growing inside is stretching you and there is no more room for growth. Spiritual leaders are imperative because they have your guide to heaven, prosperity, salvation, the road to destiny,

## *Harmonize Your Purpose!*

*faith, praying power and so much more. Generally speaking, they are your spiritual trainer and so are ones that you associate closely. So, therefore, you need to know them in the spirit, not just by looks and stuff. The key factor is your leader causing you to stretch, to have more faith and to be more developed? Indeed, many are called, but few are chosen. I have met people that will quote a word but have no value or power. Simply meaning anyone can read a word but how many can be a word? To get spiritually fit you need to hire the best spiritual trainer that can get the job done because time is a terrible thing to waste. Contractions are always painful. The more the pain the harder the labor and your labor requires more pushing power. For this birth through you, that is about to take place just remember much is*

### *Harmonize Your Purpose!*

*given, and much more is needed. If you want the birthing pains to stop, push with power!*

*The WORD in is your reproduction and multiplication as long as you have the right revelation. It teaches you and gets you spiritually fit for the journey that is bigger than you. The WORD is your manifestation and your food for all your life equations. I love to praise God especially when I'm going to feast on a Good Healthy WORD. The right WORD will gas you, and the fuel won't run out because you will know when it is time to fill back up. It will carry you with reserve. The WORD gives you the right nutrients for good nourishment, and it always replenishes because it is healthy for your soul and household. In the WORD are hidden treasures, and that will lead you to valuable artifacts which*

## *Harmonize Your Purpose!*

*are enrichment tools for your vision as well as gifts. It also nourishes which is malnourished. The WORD has many secret compartments that the world cannot comprehend to keep the values hidden. In those values is concealed peace and suppressed goods that an ordinary thinker can't understand. Peace surpasses all understanding, but it's in the WORD. Some try to perform in action as they have the WORD or pretend but soon their performance will bore you. However, you must obtain the right revelation to get the right transformation. Many false leaders are called sanctimonious praise and worship. It is contaminating the ones that trust the people and not the WORD. It is built on pretense but cannot convert. If leaders are not aligned or aligning up to the WORD, then they are called and not*

## *Harmonize Your Purpose!*

chosen. The Chosen will change because they will not be able to continue being themselves. Many signs will be shown through them that will possess the fruit of the spirit because of their secret compartments of factored viewpoints. I am pushing, but nothing is happening. If you have not seen it yet, it's coming!

So many people think they have what it takes to make something happen, but they don't. There are so many things you must get to make stuff happen. A whole new you! Yes, it sounds crazy, but it is true. To accomplish something you never had you must become someone you have never been! James 4:7 speaks of resisting the devil and he will flee. The devil is purposed to tempt you to get weak so that your future of prosperity will be held back. The temptation is allowing your

## *Harmonize Your Purpose!*

*flesh, and enticing it to feel, and emotions, not healthy pleasures. However, in this scripture, James want you to see the concepts of deception. If you resist temptations, you tap into a strength which resists. The more you resist, the stronger you become. Resistance is muscle power to allow a new force to take over. Once you grow stronger by recognizing you are – not – to remain your sight will become clearer. You will also be strengthened even in your viewpoints because what used to be out of sight will be placed in your view.*

*The more you say no, the more He can say yes. There is more power than you realize in your no but you will never know until you begin to say no. Once you act upon and stand on your no then that temptation will not be able to stir up desires that cause you to appear puny. I will*

## Harmonize Your Purpose!

never forget when I quit smoking. James 4:7 was my help. I continued to speak James 4:7 every time temptation tried to arouse me. I no longer want to look like a pathetic minister or appear fragile. The more I confessed it, the more I withdrew from smoking. I just took one day at a time and kept moving far away. I begin that fight in September 2006, and soon afterward I overcame. Life is something how we allow simple little things to keep us in bondage and away from so many beautiful things. I realized if I was going to accomplish big then I must grow big in faith and my faith needed strength it never had. Yes, the power in our no is the assurance of our faith! It also helped my faith to be able to stretch. Also, I realize how good a yes sounds after receiving so many no's.

## _Harmonize Your Purpose!_

Anytime you need to do exceedingly above all you have ever done you need a clear vision. Often many try to accomplish something impossible, and their faith is not currently at that level of all possible. It won't work. Faith is not to stay the same size or shape. A fine example of faith is like elastic it needs to be stretchable when purposed to be strong. Faith is simply limitless possibilities at all times. It must build and then be exercised. The greatest failure of faith is when one runs before time then calamity comes. Faith is something that stretches in the biggest time of need, and it's wearable though any season plus condition. It has no conditions, and it can handle all situations. It has no extreme of limits it just goes to work when one believes. Yes, it is stretchable - one size fits all! But, can you handle to ride faith as far as it

### *Harmonize Your Purpose!*

*will take you? Some could not treat religion as their eyes saw more than their faith could feel they turned back or stopped believing. Notice, faith cannot go to work if you are not willing to exercise your belief. Your belief causes faith to show up and show out. Doubt and fear will cancel out faith when one is not being strengthened to believe greater. I am pushing, but nothing is happening. If you have not seen it yet, it's coming!*

*Resistant is the power you need to build muscle in tired and weak areas of your belief. Yes, no simply makes you stronger than you can stretch as elastic becoming expandable. Resisting temptation causes you to be challenged in the area you're feeble. You cannot get an expansion until you grow large. It's time to increase your*

## Harmonize Your Purpose!

*flexibility. Elastic is a stretching with comfort and adapting to change. It builds our confidence.*

*Race needs contestants and without competitors, there is no competition. Nothing to compete for requires no race and no race no winners. Race is set for rivals to participate not in strength but endurance to achieve the many challenges ahead. It prepares one to be great in sportsmanship. Just as one appears to be a runner by looking fit, being smart, strong and so on, the real truth will be at the finish line. A contestant may look qualified but are not fit but for a mile. Others may seem well educated, but their smarts may not have an enduring power to complete the assignment. Also, some may have a proven background to be a great contestant with a great track record but still out of shape for this race.*

### _Harmonize Your Purpose!_

*One day I laughed because I was doing the right things, with the right moves, making the right decisions but in the wrong place. I thought I was in the right race. Surely, I was running but in the wrong state. Notice your competitors also help to strengthen your running power. What good is a race without competitors? Competitors are happy to have their challenge you to be a winner if you stay focused on winning. Ecclesiastes 9:11 reminds us it is more than strength, wisdom, swiftness, food, riches, or skill but the opportunity to conquer is for all. Nevertheless, stay prepared to be ready when your chance comes. It's coming, just be prepared!*

*This chapter "Run Conqueror Run," is from my book "The Birth of an Author Shall Be Born." This book will help you put an end to fear,*

## <u>Harmonize Your Purpose!</u>

*procrastination, and lost hope. It will be the epitome of everything you must succeed and you be will be a conqueror! "The Birth of An Author shall Be Born." There is a author in everyone you just must find your passion to innovate. Order today www.pariceparker.biz*

### *Harmonize Your Purpose!*

# Power to Push You

### *Parice C. Parker*

It's a joy being a part of your writing journey and I hope you continue until it's done. Your New Book deserves to live and make sure you obtain the best publishers for your book. We at Fountain of Life Publishers House would love you to come on board. If

## Harmonize Your Purpose!

we can further assist you in book publishing contact us and make sure you get that book out of you. It could be the next New York Times Best Seller or Box Office Hit.

**Fountain of Life Publisher's House** was founded in 2006 by **Parice C Parker, CEO** and author. Mrs. Parker also experienced the terrible trials of getting published. So, therefore she founded **Fountain of Life Publisher's House,** a place to "House the Voice to Speak in Print." She was gifted with a dynamic vision to help uprising authors to get published and many are finding their way to her. She works hand in hand to ensure the author's publishing journey and to help ease their book publishing process. If Parice C Parker can assist you in anyway possible to publish your book, just call or contact her. **Fountain of Life Publisher's House** is on the rise to obtain every purposed author to be birthed and guided on the right track to their destiny. We offer a wide variety of book publishing services and publishing packages just for you.

### Harmonize Your Purpose!

## *Phenomenal & Inspiring Books* ## *by Parice C Parker*

1) Living Life in A Messed Up Situation Volume One
2) Living Life in A Messed Up Situation Volume Two
3) Aggravated Assault on Your Mind
4) A Precious Gift from God
5) Word Wonders
6) The Anointing Powers of Your Hands
7) From Eating Crumbs to Transforming Wealth
8) The Birth of An Author Shall Be Born
9) Live Laugh Love & Be Happy

Visit Our Online Book Store or Where Ever Books Are Sold
www.pariceparker.biz

## *Harmonize Your Purpose!*

**Aggravated Assault on Your Mind**

Have you ever felt, the very person you have surely loved or believed in has attacked you? It may have been your closest friend, relative, child, your spouse or even yourself. Sometimes you wanted to cry and could not. Shortly afterwards, while gazing about the pain immediately tears began to fall as a flowing river. Your heart has been assaulted and snared with claws of intentions to kill. A multitude of thoughts circulate

## Harmonize Your Purpose!

in your mind and then you began to say to yourself **"How did I let this happen to me?"** Your situation was bound to occur, because somewhere along the way you have allowed your circumstance to control your mind. Allegedly, you put your trust in the wrong one or thing and then you are thrown off guard. Most definitely, you wonder, who do I blame? You did not realize you have entrusted so much of your heart to be assaulted through the passion of love you have given. A since of blindness has overwhelmed your thinking ability, rearranging your life, and throwing it off balance. Truly, there is an explanation and an apology due, but none is ever given. Certainly, you have tried to generate an effectual change. Perhaps, the more you have tried, the more your relationship seemed to die. **Instantly thinking, What Is The Use?**

## *Harmonize Your Purpose!*

### A Precious Gift from God

**Your Gift Discovery?** It teaches one the value of their natural born talent and motivates one to Live Life On Purpose! This book inspires the heart, gives courage to your *How to Ability* and causes you to live in the pursuit of your happiness. Every natural born leader needs to read this book, it is **AWE – INSPIRING!**

### Harmonize Your Purpose!

**Living Life In A Messed Up Situation**
**Volume One**

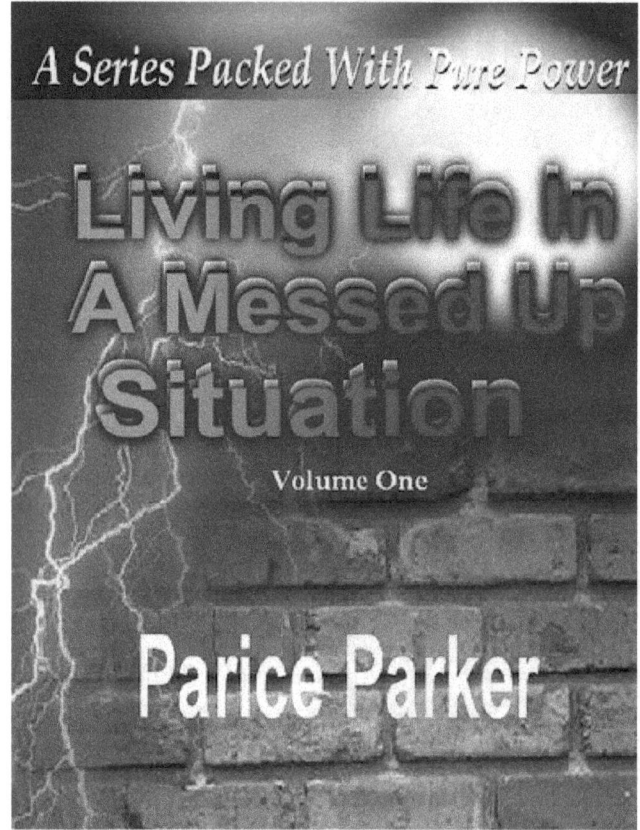

God will assign the most in-depth spiritual cleaning service through the Blood of Jesus the Christ to clean up your messed up life. **Every messed up situation that you are living** in will have a **Sparkling Effect** when God gets finished with you. Some things He dusts off, others He wipes down and some need to be

## _Harmonize Your Purpose!_

polished to shine. **Get Polished Perfect** after reading this book and simply gain it all.

### Harmonize Your Purpose!

## Living Life In A Messed Up Situation
## Volume 2

**Living Life In A Messed Up Situation Volume: Astounding ...** It seems though many things has changed within your life including your perseverance. Often you wanted to quit but couldn't afford to even STOP TRYING! As life twirled down so did your hope, dreams and prosperity. Order this book today and Reel In Your Greatest CATCH! A Mega Booster is what you need and this is it! Let JESUS catch You Trying!

## *Harmonize Your Purpose!*

### Word Wonders

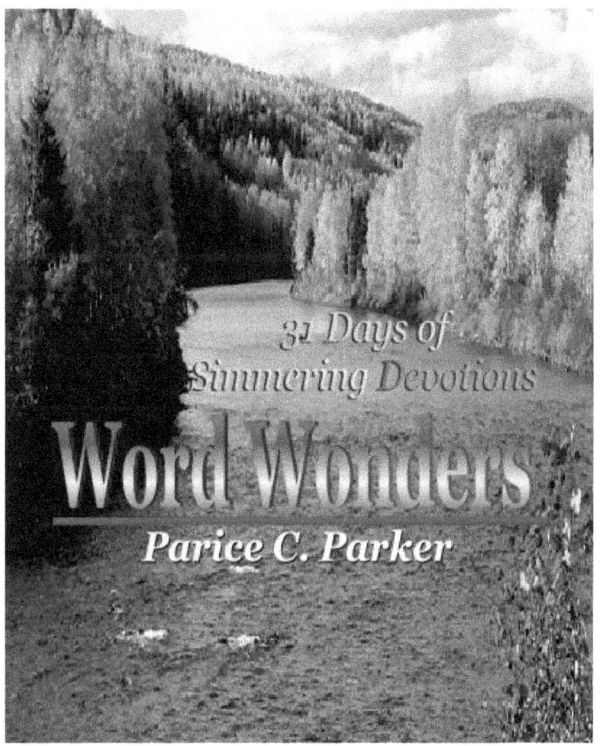

***A Eye – Opening* ...** Word Wonder inspires your HOPE to Greatly Influence your FAITH and it's a magnificent daily devotional book to help keep you focused in word. It EMPOWERS Positive Powers to cause DIVINE FAVOR to ABOUND TOWARDS YOU! Simple things you need to be equipped with more favor from on high. Get This Book TODAY!

### Harmonize Your Purpose!

## From Eating Crumbs To Transforming Wealth

***Riveting*** ... Finally, a book that keeps you in a thriving mental state that causes your HOPE to burst through! Now, it is time to identify the real you by introducing the TROPHY that is Hidden inside. It's your time to stop eating the crumbs of life and Indulge In Your WEALTHY Place!

## *Harmonize Your Purpose!*

### The Anointing Powers of Your Hands

***Absorbing*** ... Often times you wonder why, why me? Your life may not look like much right now, but keep on putting your hands to the plow of your vision and do not stop, until you perfect that thing! Working a work you have never worked can be extremely complicated and very difficult, but never quit doing the work. God want you to use what is inside you, so He can display you to the world because He Loves to be glorified! There is Anointing Powers in the working of your hands because He purposely created you. Faith without works are dead, so work it!

## Harmonize Your Purpose!

### The Birth of an Author Shall Be Born

There are great techniques for completing a book from the introduction to the end. An unfinished and unpublished book is dead. That book inside deserves to live. A lot of people wanted me to mentor them through their book writing journey because they have witnessed how I have mastered book writing. The Birth of an Author Shall Be Born is purposed to get that book out of you. Push to give your new book an opportunity to live. Someone needs your book more

## *Harmonize Your Purpose!*

than you need to write it. The Birth of an Author Shall Be Born, is it you? It's time to discover the author in you.

*Harmonize Your Purpose!*

## Fountain of Life Publishers House

P. O. Box 922612, Norcross, GA 30010
Phone: 404.936.3989

For book orders or wholesale distribution
Website: www.pariceparker.biz

*<u>Harmonize Your Purpose!</u>*

# Thank You So Much!

www.pariceparker.biz

## _Harmonize Your Purpose!_

www.ingramcontent.com/pod-product-compliance
Lightning Source LLC
Chambersburg PA
CBHW071439160426
43195CB00013B/1967